MW01626017

THEODORE CLYMER
RICHARD L. VENEZKY

Consultants
CLAIRE HENRY
DALE D. JOHNSON
HUGHES MOIR
P. DAVID PEARSON
PHYLLIS WEAVER

GINN AND COMPANY

0-663-38280-7

Acknowledgments: Grateful acknowledgment is made to Tamar Griggs for use of the poem "Here Come the Whales!" by Linda Pohwat from *There's a Sound in the Sea . . .* by Tamar Griggs. Copyright © 1975 by Tamar Griggs. Reprinted by permission.

Illustrators and photographers: Peter Bradford, cover, 4-5, 28-29; Shane Kelley, 1, border, 27; John Homes, endpaper; Richard Louie, 3, 64-65; Michael L. Pateman, 6-19, 30-43, 49-55; Gary Fujiwara, 20-21; Jeffery Rotman, 22; Ahuimanu Productions/Robert Shallenberger, 23; Miami Seaquarium, 24; Globe Photos, 25; Doug Wallin/Taurus Photos, 26; Brian Epp, 27; James Marshall, 44-48, 56-63. Photography courtesy of Miami Seaquarium for pages 6, 10, 11, 12, 13, 14, 15, 16, 17. Photography courtesy of Ocean World for pages 7, 8, 9.

Design, Ginn Reading Program:
Creative Director: Peter Bradford
Art Director: Gary Fujiwara
Design Coordinator: Anne Todd
Design: Lorraine Johnson, Linda Post, Kevin Young

Contents

Come with

Us

Ken and the Fish

"Here it is," she said.
"Come in here."

"Is a dolphin in here?" said Beth.

"Here's a dolphin," said Ana.
"Come here, dolphin!"

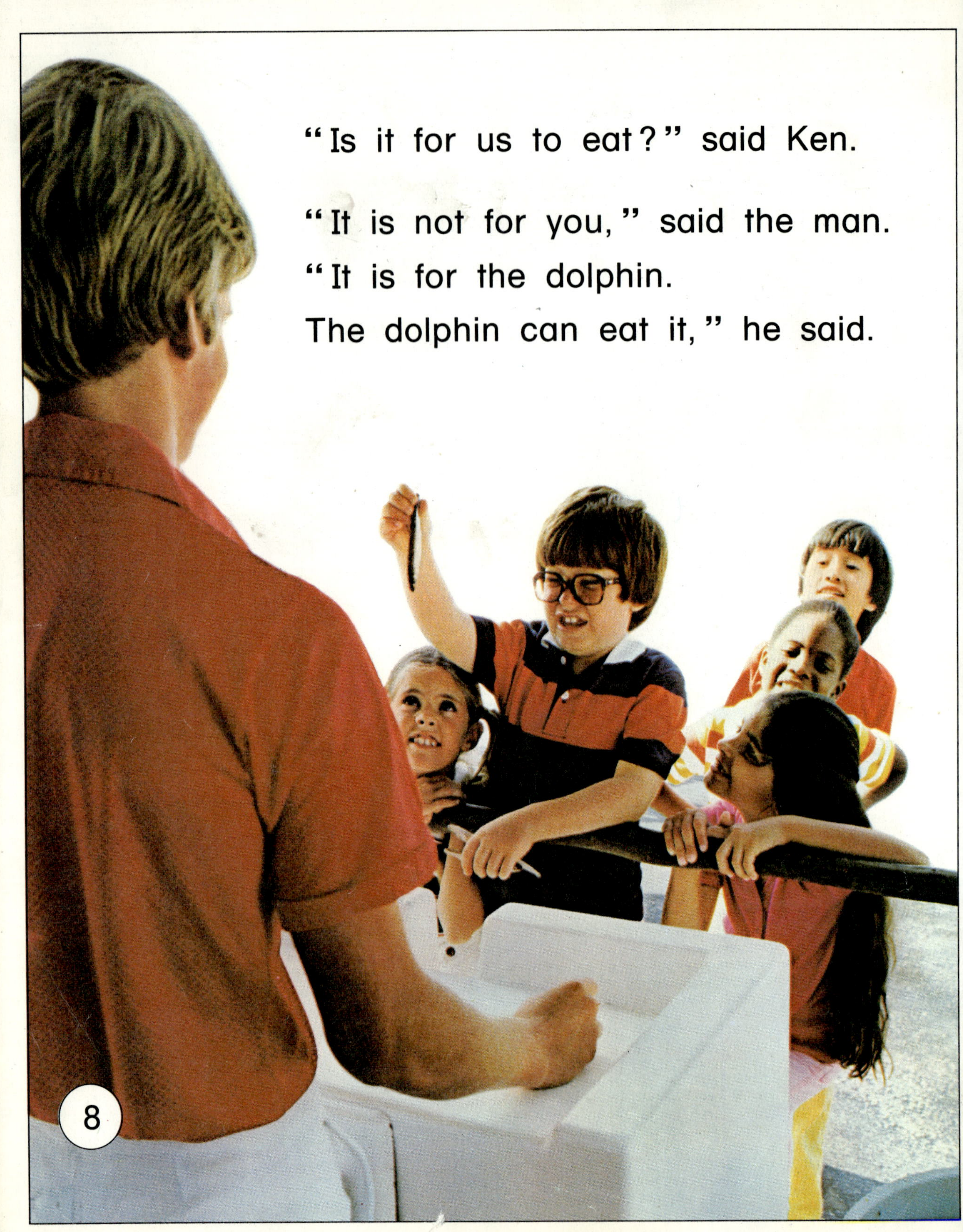

"Is it for us to eat?" said Ken.

"It is not for you," said the man. "It is for the dolphin. The dolphin can eat it," he said.

"Dolphin, here's a fish for you," said Jim. "Is the fish good to eat?"

"Look at Ken and the fish!" said Ana. "Look at the dolphin eat the fish!"

Ana and the Whale

"I can see," said Sara.

"Beth, can you see?"

"I can see the whale," said Beth.
"Look at the whale, Sara!
See the man on the whale!"

"Look at the big fish!" said Jim.

"It is not a fish!" said Ken.
"It is a whale.
Look at the big whale eat the fish."

"Look at the whale!" said Beth.
"Will the big whale get Ana?
Will it eat Ana?"

"The whale will not eat Ana," said Sara.
"It will eat a fish."

What Is It?

"Here is Mom!" said Sara.

"Come see Mom and the fish."

"Look in here," Mom said.
"Look at the big fish.
It is a shark."

"What will a shark eat?" said Jim.

"A shark will eat fish," Mom said.

"Mom, can we see this shark eat?
Can we see it eat fish?" said Sara.

"You can see this shark eat,"
Mom said.
"Look in here.
What will you see?"

"What is this?" said Beth.

"Is it a dolphin?" said Ana.

"Is it a big fish?" said Jim.

"It is Mom!" said Ken and Sara.

Here Come the Whales!

Here come the whales!
Splashing their tails!
What a sight to see!
If only I could be a whale of the sea,
It would be fun, but I'm me.

Linda Pohwat

Look at Fish

Can you see a fish in here?
Where is it?
Where is the fish?

Can you see what the big fish does?
This fish can fish for a fish.
It will eat the fish it can get.

Look at this fish.

What does it look like?

Does this fish look like a fish?

Does it look like a cat?

Where is this fish?

Is it in the water?

What is it on?

What is this in the water?

Is it a ball?

Is it a fish?

Is it a fish like a ball?

Can you play with it in the water?

What Is Here?

Mix, Make, and

Ba

ke

What Grandma Does

"Grandma!" said Ana.

"It is good to see you here!

Come here, Beth and Jim.

Come see what Grandma does."

"Look at this," said Ken.
"See what the man can make."

"I like what he can make," said Sara.

"What is this, Grandma?" said Ana.

"What does it look like?" said Grandma.

"I can see what it is!" said Jim.
"It is a van.
This van can't run!"

"Can I do it?" said Ken.
"Can I make this?"

"We will see," said the man.
"Come here.
We will see what you can do."

"Grandma, can we do this?" said Ana.

"You can," said Grandma.
"I will work with you."

"Where is Ken?" said Jim.

"He is at work with the man!" said Beth.

"I like this!" said Ken.
"Can't I do good work?
Can you make this?"

"I can't do work like this!" said the man.

Mix and Make

"We have come, Grandma," said Ana.
"We have come to work with you."

"Come in," Grandma said.

“Look in the book,” said Grandma.
“Mix this and this.”

“I can mix!” said Ken.

"Do not mix Ken in!" said Grandma.

"Mix the water in.

Make a good mix.

I will have a look at it."

“What do we do now?” said Ana.

“Make a big ball with it,” Grandma said.
“Now we can work with it.”

"Now what can we make?" said Ken.

"Make what you like," said Grandma.
"You can make a bell.
Do you like fish?
You can make a fish with this."

"See what I can make," said Ana.

"What is it?" said Beth.

"What does it look like?" said Ana.

"It looks like you!" said Beth.
"It looks like Ana!"

"I will put this in here now,"
said Grandma.

"Will you put Ana in?" said Ana.

 "I will put this Ana in," said Grandma.

“This fish looks good to eat,” said Ken.

“You can’t eat the fish!” said Grandma.

“Where is Ana?” said Ana.

“Here she is!” said Grandma.

“Mom will like this Ana!” said Ana.

CLAY TO BAKE

What You Need

You need this.

You need this.

And you need water.

What You Do

Mix this and this.

Now put in the water.

Mix and mix.

Make a clay ball.

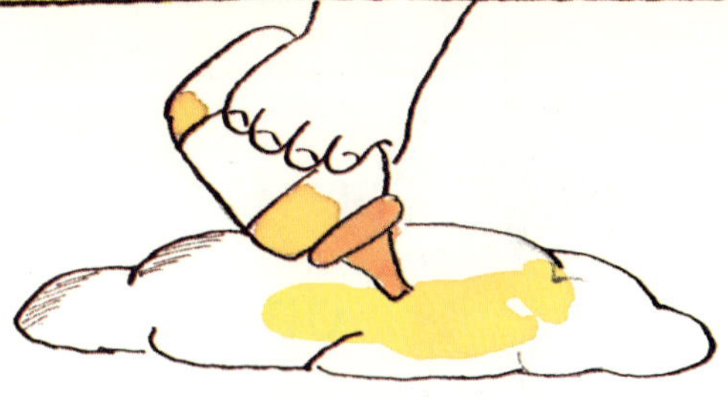

You can put this in the clay.

Do this to the clay.

Now you can do this with the clay.

You can make what you like with the clay.

You can put the clay in here.
You can bake the clay.

You do not have to bake the clay.
It does not need to bake.
You can put the clay here.

Now what do you have?
The clay looks like this.

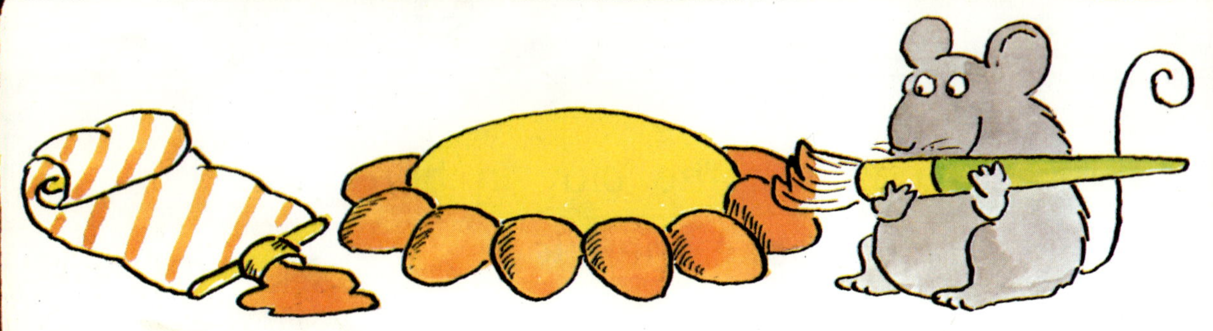

You can do this to the clay.

What can you do with it now?
Look and see.

Bread to Eat

"We have come to see you work," she said. "We have come to see you make bread."

"Come in," the man said.

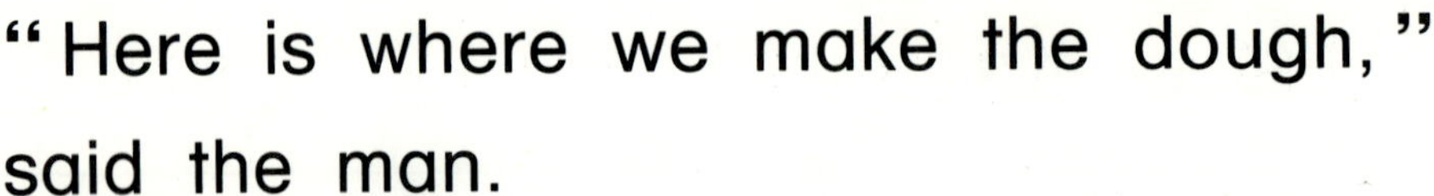

"Here is where we make the dough," said the man.

"We mix and mix to make the dough."

"Do you need water in the dough?" said Ken.

"We do," said the man.

"What is the dough here for?" said Beth.

"It has to get big now," said the man. "The dough will make a big ball."

"Here is where we make the bread," said the man.
"The dough is big now.
We can put the dough in here.
We can make the dough look like a ball.
Then we will bake it."

"Look at the dough she has," said Ana.
"The dough looks like clay.
Clay looks like bread dough.
You can't eat clay."

"You can eat this bread," said the man.

"Here is where we bake the bread,"
said the man.
"We put the dough in here.
Then it has to bake.
And then you can eat it."

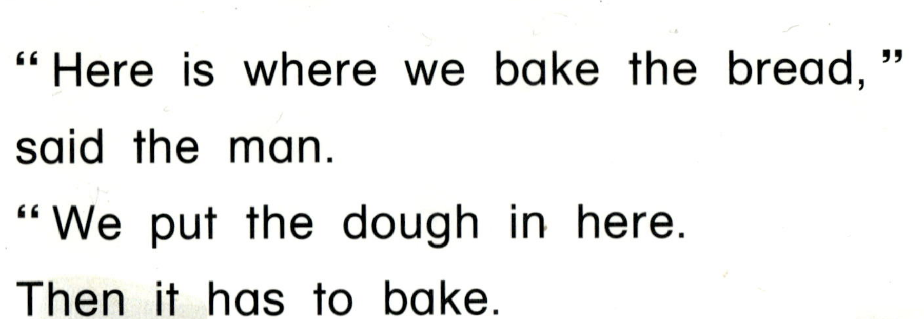

"Do you like to eat bread?" she said.
"This bread is for you.
What does it look like?"

"The bread looks like fish!" said Jim.

"This fish is good to eat," said Ken.

THE HEN AND THE BREAD

"See what I have!" said the hen.
"This will make good bread.
Who will dig?"

" Not I, " said the cat.

" Not I, " said the pig.

" Then I will, " said the hen.
And she did.

"Now we will have to cut this,"
said the hen.
"Who will cut it?
Will you cut it?"

"Not I," said the cat.

"Not I," said the pig.

"Then I will," said the hen.
And she did.

" Now who will help do this? "
said the hen.

" Not I, " said the cat.

" Not I, " said the pig.

" Then I will, " said the hen.
And she did.

"Now who will help make the dough?" said the hen.

"Not I," said the cat.

"Not I," said the pig.

"Then I will," said the hen. And she did.

"Now who will help bake the bread?" said the hen.

"Not I," said the cat.

"Not I," said the pig.

"Then I will," said the hen.
And she did.

"Now who will eat the bread?"
said the hen.

"I will," said the cat.

"I will," said the pig.

"You will not!" said the hen.
"I will!"
And she did.

Now Do This

does not

is not

do not

did not

has not

have not

can not

can

can't

Words in This Book

Level 3 introduces 37 words and maintains the 42 words introduced in Levels 1 and 2. The underlined words are introduced at this level. Words printed in second color can be decoded independently.

UNIT 1

6. here
   it
   is
   she
   said
   come
   in
7. a
   dolphin
   Beth
   here's
   Ana
8. for
   us
   to
   eat
   Ken
   not
   you
   the
   man
   can
   he
9. fish
   Jim
   good
   look
   at
   and
10. I
   see
   Sara
11. whale
   on
12. big
13. will
   get
14. Mom
15. shark
16. what
17. we
   this
22. where
23. does
24. like
25. cat
   water
26. ball
   play
   with

UNIT 2

30. Grandma
31. make
32. van
   can't
   run
33. do
34. work
36. have
37. book
   mix
39. now
40. bell
41. looks
42. put
44. need
45. clay
47. bake
49. bread
50. dough
51. has
52. then
56. hen
   who
   dig
57. pig
   did
58. cut
60. help

Words for Decoding Practice

The following words, grouped by similar elements, may be decoded independently by the pupils, utilizing the skills learned in Level 3. These groupings of words may be used to develop additional decoding lessons.

id	**ix**	**im**	**ig**	**ade**	**ame**	**ave**
bid	fix	dim	big	fade	came	cave
did	mix	him	dig	made	fame	Dave
hid	six	Jim	fig	wade	game	gave
kid		Kim	jig		lame	pave
lid		rim	pig		name	rave
rid		Tim	rig		same	save
Sid			wig		tame	wave
			zig			

CDEFGHIJ0876543

Printed in the United States of America